POSTCARD HISTORY SERIES

Swedesboro and Woolwich Township

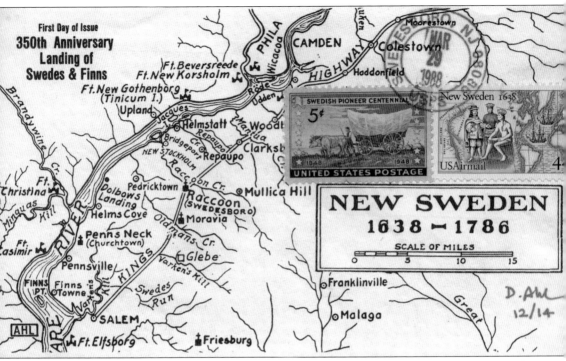

This first-day cover was circulated in honor of the 350th anniversary of the landing of the Swedish and Finnish colonists. The limited-edition cachet was produced by David H. Ahl in 1988. The New Sweden stamp was the first three-nation issue—the United States, Sweden, and Finland. The stamp was so popular it sold out in five days—more quickly than any previous United States stamp. (Courtesy Swedesboro-Woolwich Historical Society.)

ON THE FRONT COVER: In the early 1900s, farmers wait with their horse-drawn wagons on Railroad Avenue to load tomatoes onto railroad cars at the Swedesboro Station. It was said that as many as 30,000 crates of tomatoes were shipped per day by rail to many US cities. (Courtesy Swedesboro-Woolwich Historical Society.)

ON THE BACK COVER: Vanderbilt Mill was located in Woolwich Township near Auburn, New Jersey. (See page 86.) (Courtesy Swedesboro-Woolwich Historical Society.)

POSTCARD HISTORY SERIES

Swedesboro and Woolwich Township

Lois M. Stanley and Russell C. Shiveler Jr.
with the Swedesboro-Woolwich Historical Society

ARCADIA
PUBLISHING

Copyright © 2019 by Lois M. Stanley and Russell C. Shiveler Jr. with the Swedesboro-
Woolwich Historical Society
ISBN 978-1-4671-0374-9

Published by Arcadia Publishing
Charleston, South Carolina

Printed in the United States of America

Library of Congress Control Number: 2019936656

For all general information contact Arcadia Publishing at:
Telephone 843-853-2070
Fax 843-853-0044
E-mail sales@arcadiapublishing.com
For customer service and orders:
Toll-Free 1-888-313-2665

Visit us on the Internet at www.arcadiapublishing.com

*This book is dedicated to the memory of John A. Adams Jr.,
who was a passionate collector, a diligent researcher, and avid historian
of all things Swedesboro.*

CONTENTS

ACKNOWLEDGMENTS

A special note must be made to recognize John A. Adams Jr. for his determination to record the history of Swedesboro and Woolwich Township. The many postcards, photographs, and news articles accompanied by his commentary made this book possible. His foresight to will his research to the Swedesboro-Woolwich Historical Society has given the area a wealth of information for generations to come.

In addition to Jack's collected works, we thank Barbara Price and Eileen Shanahan of the Gloucester County Historical Society library for their help. Their patience in answering our endless questions was invaluable. Other assistance was given to us by Edith Rohrman, a longtime local historian. Martha and Dan Battisti provided research and much-needed technical support. Our Arcadia title manager, Caroline Anderson, guided us through the process of publication. A thank-you goes to the numerous residents who searched for postcards and photographs and combed through their memories for information.

In addition to persons, many other sources were used, specifically the libraries of the Swedesboro-Woolwich Historical Society (SWHS) and the Gloucester County Historical Society Library (GCHS). The New Jersey Archives, church and school records, old issues of the *Swedesboro News* and the *New Town Press* were helpful. The 1910 *Swedesboro Yesterday and Today* by Egee and Burk continues to be an invaluable reference. Cushing and Sheppard's 1883 *History of the Counties of Gloucester, Salem and Cumberland* was an important source. Also, William Cozen's "Origins of the Names of the Streets and Byways of Swedesboro" (2000) was beneficial.

We hope that our publication inspires readers to become more interested in our area's past and be motivated to be a part of the future of Swedesboro and Woolwich Township. Our historical society is alive and well and ready to continue collecting and preserving the past. A special interest is preserving and restoring landmarks of the area. Our mission is to provide educational programs, guided tours, and diverse exhibitions for the public.

Unless otherwise noted, all images appear courtesy of the Swedesboro-Woolwich Historical Society.

INTRODUCTION

The world is changing all of the time. Those who can meet change with acceptance will ultimately find satisfaction in the world of tomorrow. The purpose of this book is to look at the locale of Swedesboro and Woolwich Township and take stock of some of the good and some not-so-good changes that the residents have experienced. Many changes are dramatic, some traumatic, and all are occurring daily with astonishing impact. The images presented here are based on old technology: postcards and photographs. Postcards have been superseded by Facebook and Instagram. Printed photographs have been sidelined by Snapchat, and digital photographs are now carried around on cell phones.

Readers will find a theme running through the postcards and photographs that were selected to feature in this book. One of the major elements of change in the 19th century was the growth of the railroad network. Railroads first connected small towns with regional cities: Swedesboro to Camden and then to Philadelphia. Then, connections went farther from cities on the East Coast to cities in the Midwest and on to the West Coast. Freight trains delivered raw materials and new manufactured goods to small towns. Trains made people more mobile, moved resources to the points of need, and carried away tons of produce, fruits, and vegetables from places like Woolwich Township, which had an economy based on agriculture for almost 200 years after the first settlers arrived. The coming of the railroad to Swedesboro in 1869 was a transformative moment, as there followed a period of business expansion, population growth, new housing construction, and industry start-up.

The second element of change was the invention of the automobile at the beginning of the 20th century. As the use of motorized cars and trucks spread across the nation, new companies were created, and Swedesboro got its own share of new businesses. Car dealerships opened, including Reliable Garage, Homan Chevrolet, and Kingsway Motors. Fuel and service stations became part of the landscape, including Nicotra's Tydol Station, Schoener's Automotive, Atlantic Richfield gasoline, and Esso. Old byways like Kings Highway were paved. Old farms made way as new highways, such as the New Jersey Turnpike, were constructed.

Two interesting sources of postcards and photographs were well known to people locally. Edward W. Humphreys operated a photography studio in Woodstown, New Jersey, in the period 1895–1930. Humphreys did portraits of a few Swedesboro residents, including John Pierson and Miss Lucy Welsh, both of whom lived to be 100 years old. In addition to his studio work, Humphreys took his camera out and about the countryside. He collected pictures of businesses, schools, churches, and gatherings like the commemorative ceremony at the historic Moravian Church. Quiet rural scenes of lakes, farms, and gristmills such as Vanderbilt's mill and Oliphant's mill were captured by his camera lens. He sent his own photographs of scenes from Salem County and Gloucester County to outside printing firms to produce postcards. Humphreys had some of the detailed colorization work done in Germany prior to the Great War in 1914. These postcards were widely distributed throughout South Jersey.

Guest and Guest were brothers who ran a pharmacy on Main Street in Swedesboro. Their business interest turned to postcards in the early 1900s. For patrons of their store, Owen Guest and Samuel Guest produced several series of postcards, all with images taken in the Swedesboro area. Their postcards were printed abroad, some in color, some in black and white. While scenes on Guest and Guest postcards can easily be found on Kings Highway or on Railroad Avenue today, the mailing destinations also contain charming details. Some were being sent to upstate New York, or to Florida, or the Midwest. Many started the journey at the Swedesboro Post Office, which around 1907 was located at the Black building on the corner of Main Street and Lake Avenue. The Guest and Guest series included the Black building, which led to the interesting scenario of a postcard of the post office with the Swedesboro postmark.

Postcards have a hidden story too, because dating the cards with accuracy presents a challenge. This is an exercise the true collector finds fascinating. At times, the layout style changed so rapidly that a particular postcard's style can determine its production era. Prior to 1898, almost no postcards were made with local business or scenery pictures printed on either side. In that year, Congress passed a resolution to allow postcards printed with pictures, with the restriction that no message could be written on the address side. Cards also had to note that they were private mailing cards. Therefore, card makers printed photographs that occupied only 50 to 75 percent of the message side. In 1907, the law was changed so that the address side of the card could be divided in half, with the address on the right and the message on the left. This convention has continued to be used to the present. But there have been changes to the ways that colors were added or reproduced.

The postmark stamped on the cards also helps to date pictures and the year of production. If a card does not have a postmark, it can be compared to others with the same layout or same production credits. It can be frustrating to find that some postmarks only contain the month and day, but not the year. Photographs, on the other hand, are the true sphinxes of the graphic world. If no one bothered to record the names of Uncle John and Aunt Sally, and note the date, the faces just stare back from the photograph with a look of timeless mystery.

These postcards, photographs, and printed cards allow us a chance to reflect that the earlier citizens of Swedesboro and Woolwich were just as proud of their community as current residents are today. The curtain is pulled back to reveal snippets of life in Swedesboro and Woolwich. Pictures of residential neighborhoods bring a person into the setting like a casual observer seated on the front porch of the house next door. Scenes of businesses on Main Street show the hustle and bustle happening daily. The Swedesboro business community today still works hard to be attractive for residents, visitors, and the next business partner. The effort that is made to keep Kings Highway clean, to keep it decorated with banners and flowers, to make it an appealing place to work and live, should be appreciated by all.

We hope you enjoy seeing on these pages the transformation of Swedesboro and Woolwich Township in the period 1870–1950.

One

SEE THE BIG PICTURE

The Swedesboro Railroad Company, under the leadership of Joshua R. Thompson, bought the land and rights in 1867 for a 10-mile stretch of railroad through Gloucester County. Construction was completed in 1869, and the inaugural ride was made on September 16, 1869. The railroad had an immediate economic impact for the community by opening up new urban markets for Swedesboro produce.

THE FOUNTAIN, SWEDESBORO, N. J.

The Guest and Guest Pharmacy proprietors looked for creative ways to bring customers into their store on Main Street. In 1903, they rehabilitated a section of the building with a gleaming soda fountain set off by a marble countertop and wide mirrors. Elizabeth Guest was the manager of the soda shop. The store also featured a selection of Swedesboro-themed postcards, which were great sellers.

Jennings Glen Echo Fish Pond, Swedesboro, N. J.

This is a typical scene shown on Guest and Guest postcards. The Glen Echo Lake was on private property belonging to the Jennings family. Many of the postcards in this series were hand-colored, which allowed the producers to exercise some artistic license. The image here was actually taken by E.W. Humphreys, a photographer from Woodstown who also produced his own postcards of scenes in Salem and Gloucester Counties.

John Pierson was a source of boundless information about the early history of Swedesboro. He was born in 1805 in Woolwich Township and lived to be 100 years old. His public service record includes the county freeholder board, the Woolwich Township Committee, and the New Jersey General Assembly. Pierson was proudest of his accomplishments in getting many bridges built during his time as freeholder, including the iron bridge over Raccoon Creek in 1894. (Courtesy GCHS.)

Public works projects were undertaken with regularity along Raccoon Creek. Swedesboro and Woolwich Township had over 15 docks and wharves along the waterfront, as shown on a 1936 map of survey. There was a wharf for the Swedesboro Steamboat Company, which ran regular trips to Philadelphia carrying passengers and cargo.

This aerial photograph of Swedesboro dates to about 1940. Easily recognized features are the railroad, the Hurff Canning Plant, Trinity Episcopal Church, and St. Joseph's Roman Catholic Church. At this time, most of the housing construction at Pealltown and at East Avenue had been completed.

Charles D. Lippincott was a native of Harrison Township. In 1862, he enlisted in the Union army. He was discharged as a captain in 1865 at the end of the Civil War. In 1869, Lippincott and his wife moved to Swedesboro and opened a dry goods store, trading as Lippincott and Gaskill. His organizational skills were applied in the formation of local utility companies, including Woolwich Water Company and Swedesboro Heat, Light and Power Company. (Courtesy New Jersey Archives, Department of State.)

Lippincott Street was named in honor of Captain Lippincott in 1910, while he was still living. He was involved in a number of civic improvement companies, including the Lakeside Land Company. He had a remarkable skill for surveying, even though he received no formal training. Later, the name of Lippincott Street between Main and Second Streets was changed to Allen Street.

LIPPINCOTT STREET, SWEDESBORO, N. J.

Alvin Crispin rode the wave of the future, as seen in this photograph from 1905. Crispin was the first man in Gloucester County to own an automobile, as noted in the *Woodbury Constitution*. Crispin was a patient man, willing to share the roads with an endless stream of horses and wagons. He also spent much of the first day looking for a gasoline station. (Courtesy GCHS.)

Henry K. Shoemaker was a Woolwich Township boy who made the American dream come true with lots of hard work and vision. After growing up on a Woolwich Township farm, he moved into Swedesboro and bought the store at the corner of Main and Mill Streets in 1901. As a prosperous businessman, he helped found the Swedesboro Trust Company and served as the company president. He also served his country during the Great War.

Page 38

Laddtown was a tract of 30 acres laid out in building lots by Hannah Ladd in 1784. It included Water, Church, and Broad Streets. Laddtown extended all the way to Raccoon Creek on the north and to the Swedish Lutheran Church land on the east. John Ladd Sr. had purchased the property in 1714. When he died in 1741, the land passed to his son John Ladd Jr., who was the husband of Hannah Ladd. Hannah sold the lots but retained a right to collect ground rents. When she died, her nephew Samuel Mickle got the unhappy task of collecting the ground rents. His Quaker diary carefully recounts the number of trips he made from Greenwich Township to Swedesboro, his patient requests for payment of rents due, and his great frustration at the lack of cooperation from the owners of the lots.

Two

FARMS AND FIELDS

Few individuals have impacted the mail order seed business as much as W. Atlee Burpee. In 1904, Burpee purchased 81 acres in Woolwich Township for field testing new tomato and pepper varieties, and named it Sunnybrook Farm. Burpee developed the Sunnybrook pepper here, and it became one of the favorite pimento peppers. This postcard shows a pepper harvest at Sunnybrook Farm.

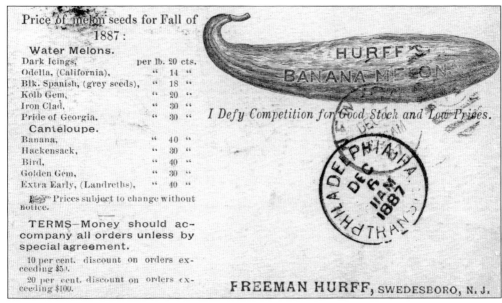

Price of melon seeds for Fall of 1887:

Water Melons.

Dark Icings,	per lb. 20 cts.	
Odella, (California),	"	14 "
Blk. Spanish, (grey seeds),	"	18 "
Kolb Gem,	"	20 "
Iron Clad,	"	30 "
Pride of Georgia.	"	30 "

Canteloupe.

Banana,	"	40 "
Hackensack,	"	30 "
Bird,	"	40 "
Golden Gem,	"	30 "
Extra Early, (Landreths),	"	40 "

☞ Prices subject to change without notice.

TERMS—Money should accompany all orders unless by special agreement.

10 per cent. discount on orders exceeding $50.
20 per cent. discount on orders exceeding $100.

I Defy Competition for Good Stock and Low Prices.

HURFF'S BANANA MELON

FREEMAN HURFF, SWEDESBORO, N. J.

As early as 1880, Freeman Hurff had launched a new business venture from his vegetable farm. He produced new varieties of watermelons and cantaloupes and started a mail order seed business. This postcard, dated 1887, was sent to a purchaser in Holland, offering seeds of six different watermelon varieties. About 1908, Hurff moved from Woolwich Township to New York State and took his business with him.

Freeman Hurff worked for over 25 years saving seeds from harvested cantaloupes and watermelons. The hardest part was getting melons this size carried from the field back to the processing house. (Just kidding.) This is a postcard spoof from Alfred Stanley Johnson. A crop that size would feed a lot of pigs!

SHIPPING SPARKS EARLIANA TOMATOES, SWEDESBORO, N.J.

The Sparks Earliana tomato variety was developed in 1900 by George Sparks, a farmer in Upper Penns Neck Township. It quickly became a favorite in South Jersey because the fruit came to full size in 60–68 days, one of the earliest to reach the East Coast markets. The shine from the skin of each perfect topper can be seen. Imagine the hundreds of tomato boxes that moved through the Swedesboro freight yard in a single day.

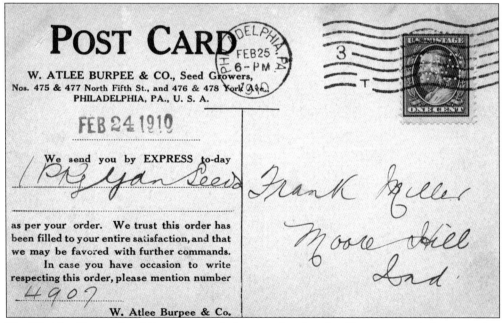

The W. Atlee Burpee Seed Company used photographs taken locally on postcards for processing orders. A postcard such as the one on page 17 for Sunnybrook Farm, or the scene above showing the shipping of Earliana tomatoes, was sent to a buyer as an order confirmation or to advise when seed packages had been mailed.

In the freight yard, laborers rest briefly from unloading sweet potatoes off the farm wagons. Sweet potatoes were loaded up in the fields using bushels, which were larger than the 5/8-bushel baskets made for picking tomatoes. In 1901, a real estate advertisement boasted that over 100,000 bushels of sweet potatoes had been loaded onto boxcars and shipped from Swedesboro.

As railway boxcars were moved onto the sidings in the freight yard, horses and wagons surged forward, and laborers appeared instantly to begin unloading vegetables. In a 1910 business directory of Swedesboro, there are 13 produce brokers listed, including J. Lewis Costello, William Conover, William H. Longacre, Frank Black, I.A. Denny, and S.W. Gaskill.

William Black owned the gristmill on Church Run until his death in 1891. After that, Hewes V. Black operated the mill in partnership with George B. Mitchell. This photograph of Black & Mitchell's mill dates to 1895. The mill wheel and raceway are hidden from view at far left.

This is an excellent view of the mill raceway. Some of the stone walls are still visible today off Franklin Street. George B. Mitchell is pictured. Mitchell bought additional equipment to generate electricity from hydropower. The mill became the primary generating station for the Swedesboro Heat, Light, and Power Company when it was founded in 1899. Naturally, Mitchell was one of the company stockholders.

Warrington's mill was a gristmill in Woolwich Township on the creek that was the township boundary. The mill was in operation before the Revolutionary War. Nathan Warrington became the owner of the mill in 1825, and his son Simeon Warrington became the owner in 1843. The mill remained in the Warrington family for 120 years.

On the road from Swedesboro to Sharptown, Oliphant's mill served farmers in both Gloucester and Salem Counties. Samuel Oliphant bought the mill in 1871 from the creditors of Robert Porch. In 1873, Samuel's son William Oliphant became the owner and operator of the gristmill. The mill survived at this location until 1964, when it was disassembled and moved to Smithville in Atlantic County.

As a farmer, Alvin Crispin had a vision of bigger harvests with less manpower. In another first for him, he is pictured here in 1906 with the first farm tractor in Gloucester County. Consider that in 1910, only 1,000 farm tractors were manufactured in the United States. The biggest share of the tractor market was held by International Harvester, which made one of every five tractors. (Courtesy GCHS.)

In July and August, the streets near the Hurff canning factory were lined with farm vehicles waiting to unload hundreds of baskets of tomatoes. If the canning plant machinery broke down, the trucks sometimes remained parked along Broad and Third Streets all night. The neighborhood closest to the plant was fragrant with the smell of tomato sauce in preparation.

14958

In addition to numerous truck farms in Woolwich Township, a number of dairy farms flourished in the Swedesboro area. Nathan Lippincott and Alvan Lippincott both bottled their own dairy products, which were delivered locally. Holstein and Guernsey cows like the ones shown here were favorite breeds because of their abundant milk production.

Alvan Lippincott purchased the Clearview Farm from his brother Nathan Lippincott in 1926. Part of the farm was lost when the New Jersey Turnpike was constructed in 1951. Alvan Lippincott maintained one of the cleanest milking parlors in Gloucester County, and his farm was often visited during the tours of the County Agricultural Board.

Earle Shiveler and Russell Shiveler contemplate the five-horsepower farm equipment on their father's farm on Oak Grove Road. The animals were named Jack, Pete, Billy, Rose, and Mae. In the late 1930s, horses were still used for pulling vegetable carts, hay loading in the field, and hay lifting into the barn. If the weather permitted, Earle enjoyed a ride in the one-horse open sleigh.

By the mid-1940s, tractors had replaced both manpower and horsepower. Here, Earle Shiveler does asparagus cultivation with a John Deere Model G tractor. The latest technology allowed one man to finish in two days the same work that would have taken two men and four horses an entire week. However, that significant increase in productivity could be quickly reversed by one flat tire.

At center is Joe Musemeci, the head of a crop-dusting service that flew out of the Bridgeport Airport. It was as thrilling as any military airshow to watch Musemeci dive and spin over the fields, then pull into a steep climb at the late minute to avoid power lines along the edge of the field. There is hardly need to explain why everyone in Gloucester County called him "Crazy Joe."

Wilbert E. and Delia P.T. Ashcraft, with their daughter Delia, are shown here on their farm on Pedricktown Road in Woolwich Township. Following his successful career in agriculture, Wilbert Ashcraft transitioned to a second act as a produce broker in Swedesboro. He owned a large warehouse on Third Street next to the freight yard.

Three

READY TO TAKE A RIDE

From earliest times, bridges over Raccoon Creek were essential to the commerce of the area. In 1887, at a cost of $4,900, a cable-stayed truss, center-bearing, swing wooden bridge was built to accommodate persons entering and leaving Swedesboro. Stone Meeting House Road crossed the creek over the farmland of Ben Richardson to Francis Street—now known as Richardson Avenue.

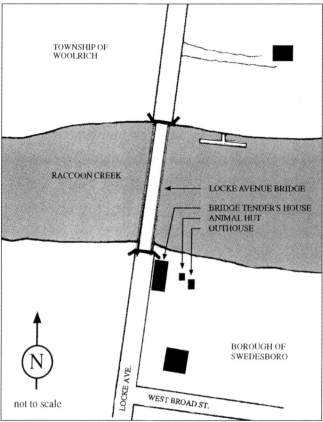

The early bridge had to be opened manually. Boatmen had to leave their vessels to open the bridge and enable passage. Due to the labor and time involved, captains threatened to leave the bridge open. The need for a bridge tender was recognized. In 1890, a shelter was built for a person who was paid $25 a month to open and close the bridge. The house on the south side of the bridge was home to five men over the years. The one-story, gable-roofed structure of three rooms remained until it and the later 1911 bridge were demolished. At one time, it was enlarged to accommodate the tender's wife and a small store. Through the years, this bridge was commonly called a drawbridge and the road was known as Drawbridge Road. It is now known as Locke Avenue.

Starting in the late 1930s, Peter K. Leap was in charge of the bridge for about 15 years. Due to a decrease of traffic on the creek, he began to trap snappers and net fish. When he had a sufficient number of carp, he sold them to a trucker from New York City. Pete and his faithful German shepherd were often seen walking around town. (Courtesy GCHS.)

The current Locke Avenue Bridge was opened on May 9, 2004. It replaced a nearly 100-year-old single-lane structure that crossed Raccoon Creek. The old bridge was eligible for the National Register of Historic Places, but funds were not available to preserve the structure. The bridge is used by motorists as a shortcut to areas south of Swedesboro.

TOLL GATE.
11976 Swedesboro, N.J.
Pub by Guest & Guest

By 1859, main roads were designated and tollgate houses erected in order to collect road tax money. Rates were determined by the type of vehicle, such as carriages, sleighs, carts, and sleds. One cent was charged for the vehicle and the animal. Additional pennies were charged for each additional animal. Herded sheep, goats, and cattle were counted by the dozen. A mill, which was less than a cent, was payment for the herd. Passage for those attending church and funeral services and those going to mills was free. The tollgate pictured here was located at the corner of Kings Highway and Paulsboro Road. In the view below looking north in 1875, gatekeeper Thomas Kirby and his family, who lived in the gatehouse, are pictured.

Across Raccoon Creek at Kings Highway is a bridge that has always been the main access to town. An 1826 covered bridge at this location was set on fire by a firecracker. A new truss-type bridge was completed at a cost of $2,061.20 in 1829. Heavy rains often flooded the area. In 1894, the iron bridge pictured was erected by John Pierson, the Gloucester County bridge builder. The present cement span was built in 1942 after a devastating flood caused the dam at Lake Narraticon to break.

HARRY JUSTICE
RIVER RD. R·F·D #2
SWEDESBORO·N·J·

Harry Justice's Sunoco station was located on River Road, the old name for Crown Point Road. Above, the owner stands proudly in front of his Blue Ribbon Service Station. Coca-Cola and Breyers ice cream are advertised. Small, full-service stations were prevalent up to the advent of supersized modern ones such as Wawa. In addition, all small towns had several stations that provided tobacco products, candy, and hand-dipped ice cream. Favorites with children were the small Dixie ice-cream cups with collectible celebrity lids. Harry Justice was ahead of his time by mailing advertising postcards to local residents.

Dear Neighbor -
Do you recognize picture? It's here you get real personal service and the most for your money.
You can't buy inferior, cut price Guess-olines here. We recommend only Blue Sunoco —
Today's Biggest Gasoline Value

Mr. Walter Storicks,
Bridgeport, N. J.

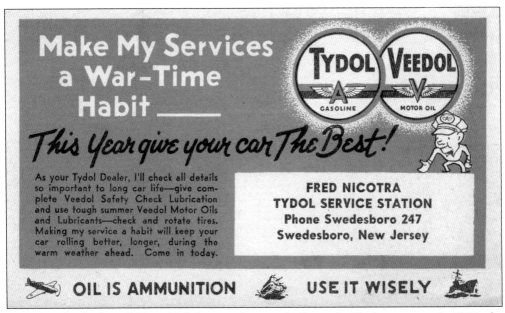

Sometime in the late 1920s, a Tydol gas station was built on the Rode property. In 1968, the Rode family gave the Tydol Oil Company a 20-year lease on the property. In 1969, the oil company demolished the structure. The postcard advertisement notes that Fred Nicotra was the owner of the newly built facility. The now empty building stands as a reminder of what was once a busy corner.

Swedesboro Interchange on the New Jersey Turnpike

The first 53-mile stretch of the New Jersey Turnpike, from Bordentown to Deepwater, officially opened on November 5, 1951. Ceremonies at Interchange 2 on Route 322 included the Swedesboro High School Band under the direction of Mary Ann Homan. Local dignitaries attending were Swedesboro mayor Earl Erdner, Woolwich committee chair Mayhew Davidson, and Freeholder Henry Salisbury.

The New Jersey Railroad Passenger Locomotive No. 44 was a typical steam engine used on the trip from Woodbury to Swedesboro in 1869. These smaller engines were built for shorter hauls and lighter railcars. In the first year of operation, the Swedesboro Railroad Company was proud to report that 2,000 passengers had traveled its rails. As increasing numbers of freight cars were added, a change was made to use heavier locomotives on the line.

Born in Woolwich in 1845, Isaac Hurff Weatherby was an engaging gentleman farmer. He farmed over 200 acres on Old Ferry Road until 1877, when he relocated to a smaller farm next to the freight yards at Swedesboro. Weatherby had a passion for cultivating new vegetable plants, both for traits of productivity and for size. The look of pride on his face as he carries a trophy watermelon in from the field is unmistakable.

This building was the main passenger station at Swedesboro. It was located between Railroad Avenue and Allen Street. To the right of the station are several warehouses along Third Street. Until Swedesboro built its own high school in 1923, several students rode the train up to Woodbury to attend school each day. The station was still standing in 1984; passenger traffic had ceased decades earlier.

The freight station was a long, narrow shed located between Railroad and Grant Avenues. It took several laborers to move hundreds of barrels, boxes, and crates from the building to the freight cars daily. The rail yard was also surrounded by several factory buildings where wooden barrels and packing boxes were manufactured for shipping containers.

Freight Station, Swedesboro, N. J.

All these freight cars would start the day on the sidings, waiting for the farm wagons to arrive. The main tracks are just out of sight on the left. Then, as horses and wagons jostled for position and the sun rose and grew hotter, so did the swarm of activity. All were impatient to unload and head back to the farm, where more produce was already being packed. Until late in November, after the last sweet potatoes had been harvested and shipped, the freight yard remained a busy area.

By 1913, all the smaller railroad companies across South Jersey had disappeared. The West Jersey and Seashore Railroad was operating all passenger and freight trains from Camden to Atlantic City to Cape May. Nine trains each day departed from Woodbury and arrived in Swedesboro in about 30 minutes. From Swedesboro, the trains continued to Alloway Junction, and then to Salem.

If necessary, trains will wait five minutes at junction points in the State of New Jersey for advertised connecting trains.

PENNSYLVANIA RAILROAD.
West Jersey & Seashore Railroad.

SALEM BRANCH—ELMER AND QUINTON BRANCHES.

Schedule in effect May 25, 1913.—(Revised.)

Eastern Standard Time.   The time between 12 o'clock, noon, and 12 o'clock, midnight, is indicated by heavy-faced type.

None of the electric trains will be held more than three minutes at Camden for boat connections, except the 11.55 P. M. Saturday only train.   ◊ Electric trains.   ● Runs week-days, except Saturdays.   ♦ Steam trains.   * Runs Saturdays only.   ♦ On Saturdays leaves at 4.59 P. M.   Y Indicates that no baggage car is attached to the train between Philadelphia and Glassboro.   "c" Regular stop only to receive passengers.   "f" Stops only on signal or notice to Agent or Conductor to receive or discharge passengers.   X Indicates that no baggage car is attached to the train between Philadelphia and Woodbury.

Form 26.   1000.   5-27-13.   1st ed.

LIPPINCOTT STREET, SWEDESBORO, N. J.

The first location of Reliable Garage was the building on the left on Lippincott Street. J. Willard Shoemaker, the son of Henry K. Shoemaker, was the man who started the Ford sales office and repair center. There was also a curbside gasoline pump. Reliable Garage later moved to the corner of Second Street and Locke Avenue in the 1960s.

You are cordially invited to inspect the

New *Ford* Car
THE UNIVERSAL CAR

now on display at our show room

Reliable Garage

J. W. Shoemaker, Prop.   Swedesboro, N. J.

J. Willard Shoemaker was not just any ordinary business owner; he was a great lover of automobiles and an excellent mechanic. He made Reliable Garage the place where Ford car and truck lovers came to buy vehicles for over 40 years. Sadly, Shoemaker was killed in a roadside accident in 1934 while he was out on a service call on a rainy evening. His passing was a great shock to the community.

This garage was built by William H. Longacre in 1925 on land purchased in 1922. It later became the location of the Homan Chevrolet automobile dealership. This was on the old borough property where, in 1902, there had been a small jail building and the fire tower. When the new borough hall was built, the fire tower was moved across Main Street and the jail building was sold to the Borough of Pitman.

The Swedesboro Glass Works began operations in May 1885. Because of the summer heat, the factory usually closed from late May to early October. There was an influx of workers who arrived in the borough, some coming from nearby plants in Glassboro, Clayton, and Millville. The skilled glassblowers in the 1900 census included brothers Adam and David Frederick and brothers Charles and Ferdinand Andorfer.

Winter fun was enjoyed at a lake near West Point, New York. Swedesboro residents Constantine and Martha Damask and Dorothy and Clarence Gahrs take a moment to rest on this icy davenport sculpture during a weekend trip to the Hudson River valley. The Damasks and the Gahrs were neighbors on Park Avenue in the 1940s, and lifelong friends. (Courtesy Doug Damask.)

During the mobilization for World War II, many of the servicemen from the Swedesboro area went for training at the Fort Dix Army Base. Here are two concerned parents, Ben Norton and Walter Shiveler, visiting on the weekend while their sons were doing basic training. Of Shiveler's seven sons, four served in the armed forces. Of Norton's three children, one son and one daughter volunteered in the cause. (Courtesy Donna Paranto.)

On Sunday afternoons, an allowance was made for families to visit and share with cousins, aunts, and uncles. Here, Lillian Shiveler has brought her family for a visit with her sister Anna Norton at the Center Square schoolhouse. In the front row are, from left to right, Charles Norton, Archer Shiveler, and Edith Norton. In the back row are Walter Shiveler Jr., Ben Norton, Anna Norton, Marie Shiveler, Russell Shiveler, Helen Shiveler, Ruth Shiveler, Lillian Shiveler, and Walter Shiveler Sr. (Courtesy Donna Paranto.)

The Chester–Bridgeport Ferry crossed the Delaware River, with its first customers in 1930. It became a connecting point for Swedesboro residents taking leisurely rides to Wilmington or to Lancaster County. Headed in the opposite direction, there came a lot of traffic from Pennsylvania through Swedesboro on the way to the Jersey Shore.

In 1909, Bethesda Methodist Church had an Epley pipe organ installed for its worship services. George Ashton was the organist there for almost 30 years. Ashton was so appreciative of the musical range of the organ that he often agreed to perform on Sunday evenings, with a mixture of spiritual and popular songs. His recitals drew music lovers from all parts of Gloucester County. (Courtesy GCHS.)

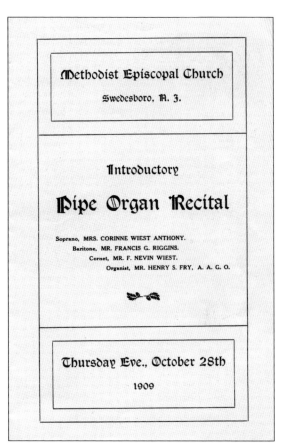

Methodist Episcopal Church

Swedesboro, N. J.

Introductory

Pipe Organ Recital

Soprano, MRS. CORINNE WIEST ANTHONY.
Baritone, MR. FRANCIS G. RIGGINS.
Cornet, MR. F. NEVIN WIEST.
Organist, MR. HENRY S. FRY, A. A. G. O.

Thursday Eve., October 28th

1909

The Swedesboro Auction continued a tradition of bringing together the farmers and the buyers and sending the produce on its way to distant markets. One thing that never seemed to change was the hours spent waiting in line for all the transactions to take place. Truck sitters would pass the time sharing the latest farm reports, or perhaps some local gossip, or else fortify themselves with a bestselling novel. (Courtesy Swedesboro Auction.)

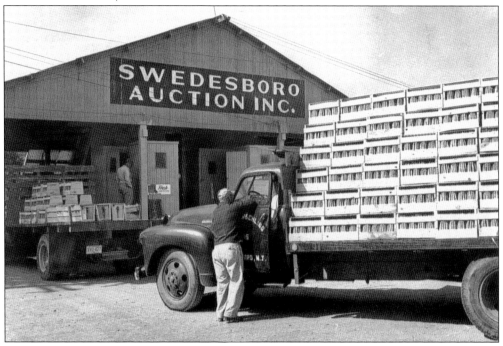

Woolwich Township Hall was first a place to house the municipal departments and records. It also hosted the township committee and the municipal court. The Swedesboro Grange shared the facility for its regular meetings. This Grange photograph shows, from left to right, (first row) Betty Hunt, a Mrs. Coles, Kate Butler, Marie Hunt, Evelyn Packer, and Ruth Jordan; (second row) Donald Hunt, Carlton Coles, George Shiveler, Laurence Hunt, Ken Stretch, Russell Shiveler, Howard Packer, Rev. Parker Auten, Walter Shiveler, Clarence Butler, and John Sharp.

In 1927, Carmelo LaRosa purchased the house at the corner of Kings Highway and Old Ferry Road and added a new building, which became his country store and gasoline service station. The house was part of a farm owned by Clarkson Ogden up until 1901. The Ogden family had lived in the area since the early 1800s.

COWTOWN SATURDAY NIGHT RODEO – MAY 25–AUG. 31 – 7:30 P.M. EDST

Cowtown Rodeo in Sharptown, New Jersey, offered good family entertainment, live spectacle, and a taste of the Old West. All this was available within a few easy driving miles from Swedesboro on a Saturday night. This postcard has a personal invitation from Howard Harris III to experience the championship level of competition of man vs. beast. The rodeo always had an element of the unexpected, along with a good dose of humor from the rodeo clowns. The many pastures and pens at Cowtown allowed some close-up viewing of farm livestock, including Brahma bulls, steers, and racehorses. The crowd often cheered for hometown favorites from Salem County.

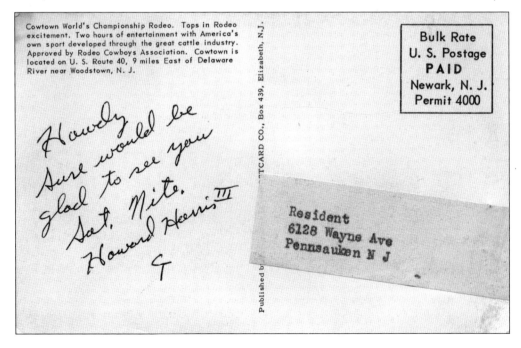

Cowtown World's Championship Rodeo. Tops in Rodeo excitement. Two hours of entertainment with America's own sport developed through the great cattle industry. Approved by Rodeo Cowboys Association. Cowtown is located on U. S. Route 40, 9 miles East of Delaware River near Woodstown, N. J.

TCARD CO., Box 439, Elizabeth, N.J.

Published b

Bulk Rate
U. S. Postage
PAID
Newark, N. J.
Permit 4000

Howdy
Sure would be
glad to see you
Sat. Nite.
Howard Harris III

Resident
6128 Wayne Ave
Pennsauken N J

'Mid the Dairy Farms of Southern Jersey
The Home of Richman's Country Fresh Ice Cream

Is there a better way to celebrate summer than an evening treat of a bowl of ice cream? Richman's restaurant in Sharptown offered all flavors of ice cream imaginable. Originally, in 1894, the ice cream was manufactured by hand. The Richman's facility included the food manufacturing plant, a service window for hand-dipped ice cream, a restaurant for full dinners, and an upstairs ballroom for special catered receptions.

PARK FRONT, RIVER VIEW BEACH, Pennsville, N. J.

Riverview Beach Park in Pennsville, New Jersey, could be reached by boat or by automobile. The Wilson Line brought passengers from Wilmington for a full day of riding the amusements. This amusement park was visited by many Swedesboro residents because of its proximity. The ride through the Salem County countryside was very relaxing, and the park offered a low-tech form of air-conditioning—cool breezes off the Delaware River.

44

RIVERVIEW PARK

Riverview Beach Park had several rides that enthralled its young visitors. The carousel had a special attraction because it could be enjoyed by all ages. It was one of the last rides to remain open to the public. Another favorite ride was the Mule Train. Many youngsters feared getting tossed when these animatronic critters turned into bucking broncos. Among the amenities at the park was a fully lined, concrete swimming pool. For people who only knew about swimming in farm ponds or at Lake Narraticon, the Riverview pool was in another class of luxury.

NEW $150,000 POOL, RIVERVIEW BEACH, PENNSVILLE, N. J.

Pool 75x150 feet with 60,000 gallons of purified water per hour. Spacious clean, white sand beaches, handball courts, modern lockers, hot and cold showers. Everything for the comfort of patrons. Brilliantly lighted at night. Guards constantly on duty. The pool and equipment has no equal in this part of the country.

Tobogan Slide Alcyon Park

Another amusement park close to Swedesboro was Alcyon Park in Pitman. In 1905, a visitor could take a heart-pounding ride on the Tobogan Slide roller coaster. More tranquil offerings were boat rides on the lake or a twirl on the carousel. Over the years, the amusement rides gave way to a car racing track. Car racing events were held at Alcyon up until 1960.

THE RIALTO WOODBURY NJ - 1697

Although Swedesboro had its own theater for movies, there was also the Rialto Theater in Woodbury as an alternate. Often, the Rialto had first-run movies, which appeared there several weeks before appearing at the Embassy Theater. It also had the advantage that a young couple might enjoy a date without being recognized by friends and neighbors at the local picture show.

Four

SIGHTS ON MAIN STREET

At the center of this postcard is the horse watering basin that was dedicated to the memory of John C. Rulon. In addition to his job as head teller at the Swedesboro National Bank, he was a stockholder in the water, sewer, and utility companies that were formed in response to the town's growth in the late 1890s.

Traveling south on Main Street, one could not miss the imposing three-story Clark's Hotel. The Sheaf of Wheat tavern was located at the site as early as 1815. Benjamin Clark built the structure shown here around 1885 and operated it as proprietor until 1910. After his death, the Clark family leased the hotel to John P. McIntyre.

This postcard dates to 1922, when Harry Ford took over the hotel. There is a preprinted message on the back advising visitors to Swedesboro that Ford's Hotel offered a Sunday special chicken dinner for hungry weekend travelers.

SWEDESBORO HOTEL ON ROUTE TO NEW CASTLE FERRY, SWEDESBORO, N. J.

Black's Post Office Block, Swedesboro, New Jersey.

This building at the corner of Lake Avenue and Main Street was built in 1906 by Hewes V. Black. The post office moved here from the Justice house, a few doors away. At one time, there was also the dentist office of Dr. W.P. Luffberry on the first floor, as well as a pool hall. The post office remained here until 1940, when it moved across Main Street to Hunt Hall.

Swedesboro Trust Co., and Main Street, Swedesboro, N. J.

In 1914, the Swedesboro Trust Company opened for business at this building, where it competed for customer deposits with the Swedesboro National Bank. The Swedesboro National Bank suffered financial difficulties in the late 1930s. Swedesboro Trust Company took over the accounts of the bank and relocated to the larger bank building on the west side of Main Street.

Before Altman Brothers moved into the Ashton & Crispin building in 1945, the first floor was occupied by the American Stores. In that year, the Hendrickson building across the street was demolished, and American Stores moved there. It was later renamed the Acme Store.

Ulysses Estilow moved to the location of Madara Brothers store in 1932. He operated a hardware store and a men's clothing store at this space until his death in 1965. Estilow was a great collector of Abraham Lincoln memorabilia and encouraged patrons to examine his cases with Lincoln's pictures and writings. As a local scholar, Estilow was often called upon as a lecturer and enthralled people with stories about the 16th president.

Founded in 1883, the Swedesboro National Bank first operated out of space in the Hannold building. The bank purchased a lot for $600 from John C. Rulon, next to his home on Main Street. That same year, this modest brick structure was completed in 90 days, at a thrifty cost of only $5,000. This new location for the bank near Railroad Avenue became a hub of activity in town.

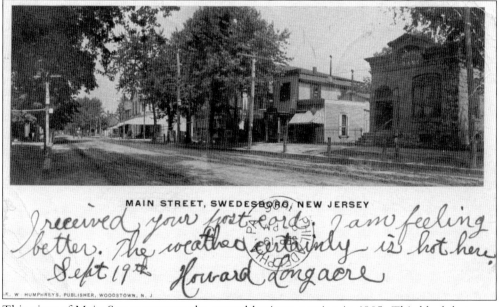

This view of Main Street captures the central business portion in 1905. This block between Mill and Lake Streets contained the drugstore, the Madara grocery store, the barbershop, the jewelry store, Swedesboro National Bank, and the post office. People could get almost all their business done without even needing to cross the street.

George Madara stands outside of Madara Brothers grocery store on Main Street, about 1910. The watermelons and assorted vegetables would be freshly picked on nearby farms in Woolwich Township and delivered before the market opening. George died in 1917 from a lingering illness. His brother Louis Madara continued to run the store as a sole proprietor, but the business still traded as Madara Brothers.

Madara Brothers used postcards to advertise the store as the "Wide Awake Grocers." This bouquet of carnations may have been a subliminal reminder of the freshness of food available at the store, which opened in 1904. While still in their teens, the brothers had both worked as clerks at another store before opening their own business. Their competition on Main Street was from H.K. Shoemaker. The Madara Brothers grocery store closed in 1931.

Eight of the workers at H.K. Shoemaker General Store are, from right to left, (first row) Eva Estilow, Laura Hawn, Ed Hawn, and Earl Casey; (second row) Bert Orr, U.S. Estilow, Harry Cottrell, and Benezet Decker, wearing the vest. Seated at far left is store visitor Charles LeCroy. The variety of items available at Shoemakers has its parallel in the Walmart superstores of today.

Up close, one can see how large the H.K. Shoemaker building was. In 1905, Shoemaker occupied both units of this duplex. Stores filled the first-floor rooms, with apartments on the second and third floors. The large wrought iron fire escape was fabricated locally at the C.B. Decker foundry.

Beginning in 1910, William G. Hanson operated a store in the Groff building that offered men's and women's apparel. His son Horace Hanson took over in 1914 as proprietor of the store and remained in business there until 1929. Horace also worked at the Swedesboro National Bank for several years as a teller and served the borough in an official capacity as tax collector.

This postcard from 1913 shows a view looking south along Main Street. On the left is the Samuel Groff building with the clothing store of William G. Hanson, who was a nephew of Groff. Next was the home and office of Dr. Benjamin Buzby, who practiced medicine in the borough from 1890 until he retired in 1940. The next building visible is the Howell building.

Albert Talman operated this shop for boots and shoes on Main Street in Swedesboro in 1905. He took over the business from his father, who was making footwear in Swedesboro as early as 1840. In 1940, William W. Talman, grandson of the founder, still operated the shoe business—although by that time, shoes were no longer being made locally by hand.

In 1874, George T. Ford purchased the old tavern and property at the corner of Main Street and Ashton Avenue. Ford demolished the old building and replaced it with a new hotel. This postcard dates to 1914, when H.K. Shoemaker had a car dealership in one half of the first floor. Ford's Hotel lived through various reincarnations and business ventures, including a package goods store and a fine dining restaurant trading as Old Swedes Inn.

Clifford L. Pither lived his whole life in Swedesboro. His grandfather George M. Pither had moved from South Carolina to be the printer of the *Swedesboro News*. Clifford worked many years as a printer, and learned the craft from his father, George W. Pither. Clifford served for a time in the 1940s as the municipal judge, but in 1946 he returned to his newspaper roots, writing a column titled "Headline Hunting with Boys around the Stove."

This is White's Drug Store, located at the corner of Main and Franklin Streets. Guest and Guest sold the building in 1920 to Charles White, a graduate of the Philadelphia College of Pharmacy and Science. After White died, his wife was the proprietor of a variety store at this location. The woman in the photograph is Ella Gebhard, a sister of Emma White.

The small building seen on the right in this photograph from 1905 was the jewelry store of Jedediah James. He took over the business when his uncle Israel James died in 1898. By 1930, James had moved the jewelry store to Pitman. The store at center was a barbershop owned by Lewis C. Headley. As a young man, Headley had learned the art of cigar rolling and offered his customers some homemade stogies.

Percy McCollister and his family moved from Woodbury to Swedesboro about 1918 and lived in this house. His father, Harry C. McCollister, was a music teacher; his mother was a daughter of Benjamin C. Clark and received a significant inheritance from her father. Percy was the assistant postmaster at Swedesboro in 1942.

On Market Day in Swedesboro, horse-drawn wagons loaded with farm produce far outnumbered automobiles on Main Street. This picture was taken from the front yard of Clark's Hotel at the intersection of Main Street and Auburn Avenue. Farm wagons would have stretched all the way from the railroad yard, along Railroad Avenue and Main Street, and continued for some distance on Auburn Avenue.

MAIN STREET, SWEDESBORO, N. J.

This view of Main Street shows the level of activity in the central business area. The time frame is about 1935. In the store at center, Madara's Market has been taken over by William Freihon. The general store and grocery store of H.K. Shoemaker has been taken over by George Weatherby and Eli Stewart.

Five

VIEW FROM THE FRONT PORCH

The Hatton house was built in 1767 by John Hatton, an unpopular collector of taxes and customs for the king of England. After the British army evacuated Philadelphia in 1778, he fled the country. His house was seized by special commissioners and sold the same year. In 1812, it was sold to John Welsh, whose family lived there until 1912. Lucy Welsh, one of the last surviving members of the Welsh family, was much more beloved in Swedesboro than Hatton had been.

The Stratton mansion has all the elements of a grand country estate. Dr. James Stratton started construction in 1793 and spared no expense to finish the building. Originally, the house was set on 600 acres, just about 100 yards off the major north–south highway. Gov. Charles C. Stratton was born in and died in an upstairs bedroom.

1899
Robert Rainey farm
Vanderbuilt Mill Rd
left to his son
John Rainey

The windmill at the Robert H. Rainey farm on Vanderbilt Road was a local landmark, which disappeared from the landscape just a few years ago. Robert bought the 110-acre farm in 1899. He was a very successful farmer, as were his brothers William and Hugh Rainey, who owned adjacent farms. The Rainey family immigrated from Ireland in 1865.

Dr. Luther F. Halsey married Catherine Murphy, a local girl, and moved to Swedesboro in 1858. When the Civil War started, Dr. Halsey and Dr. Charles Garrison debated which of the physicians should offer services to the Union army. Dr. Halsey, being the younger of the two, decided to join the army. He survived the war and was an officer at the local Grand Army of the Republic veterans' association. (Courtesy GCHS.)

The house at far left, located at the corner of Grant Avenue and Main Street, was sold in 1858 by John L. Grant to Dr. Luther F. Halsey. Dr. Halsey maintained his practice here for almost 40 years. The house on the opposite corner was built by Amos Hurff in 1895. Incidentally, Grant Avenue is named for the former owner, and not for President Grant.

WEATHERBY MANSION.
Property of the Swedesboro Land Association.
For Sale for the next ten days at $4,000—terms to suit.

The house shown here is the old Weatherby mansion located off Broad Street. In 1877, Isaac Hurff Weatherby purchased 50 acres between Locke Avenue and Raccoon Creek from the three Vanneman brothers—Isaac, Charles, and Helms. In 1903, this same land was sold by Edward Anderson of Philadelphia to the Swedesboro Land Company, and house lots were already laid out for this section of Swedesboro, which became known as Pealltown.

These houses along Vanneman Avenue between Helms Avenue and Broad Street were all built around 1905. The first house was owned by Elizabeth Kirby. The second was owned by I. Newton Hannold, who succeeded his father as the proprietor of the furniture store on Main Street. The family of Clinton B.F. Black lived in the third house. Black ran a business as a produce commission merchant.

The section of Swedesboro known as Pealltown was built beginning in 1903 on the farm of I.H. Weatherby. A new street laid out in this neighborhood was named to honor Weatherby, who had been an officer of Swedesboro National Bank and had encouraged business and residential construction in Swedesboro.

This grand Victorian home at the corner of Helms and Weatherby Avenues was owned by Mr. and Mrs. W. Harold Homan from 1928 to 1972. The Homans purchased the house from the original owner, Wilbur K. Sloan, who was editor of the *Swedesboro News* in the 1920s. Sloan chose such a large house wisely because he lived under the same roof with his in-laws for 14 years.

This house at the corner of Broad Street and Vanneman Avenue was one of the first built in the new Pealltown section of Swedesboro. Many of the homes along Broad Street were purchased by workers at the Swedesboro Glass Works. One hopes they had considered the danger of living so close to the plant, as there were several small fires that occurred there before the destructive fire of 1912.

This block of houses on Railroad Avenue between Main and Second Streets is still standing, except for the first one. This one was owned by George B. Mitchell, and was removed when the bank expanded its parking lot. Most of the Victorian gingerbread on the Railroad Avenue homes has been removed. The peaceful scene here fails to capture the hustle and bustle of the farm wagons heading to the railroad freight station and produce warehouses.

Houses were built along Second Street as early as the 1830s. This section marked the transition from Laddtown homes, closest to Raccoon Creek, to the houses built on the old James plantation tract. The angle on Second Street near Allen Street marks the beginning of the Laddtown section.

Houses on Allen Street did not have the same number of traffic problems as Main Street or Railroad Avenue. However, the proximity of the rail yard meant there was always noise from locomotive steam engines, whistles, and screeching brakes. One advantage was that living here made it easy to catch the train on time.

The architectural style in the Pealltown section began with modest two-story, single-family houses and even some double houses along Broad Street. By 1905, some of the largest three-story homes were being constructed along Helms and Anderson Avenues. As construction wrapped up in 1912, some smaller houses were filling in the remaining lots, such as this one-story bungalow at the corner of Helms and Vanneman Avenues.

The lots along East Avenue were laid out in 1900 by the Lakeside Land Company. In 1902, John C. Helms moved from Bridgeport to Swedesboro into the large house he built at the corner of Main Street and East Avenue on land that he bought from the company. The tract of 15 acres extending from Main Street to the lake was originally raw land owned by Dr. Charles Garrison. In his will dated 1871, he devised the property to his daughter Frances S. Thompson. In 1899, her executors sold the tract to the Lakeside Land Company.

SWEDESBORO, N. J.   East Ave. and Thompson St.

Because of the number of houses that were constructed in the Victorian style in the early 1900s, the turret room on every house alone is enough to make it stand apart from other houses in town. One of the largest turret rooms was constructed on this house at East Avenue and Thompson Street. Henry Ridgeway bought several lots from the Lakeside Land Company and sold them with houses to the first owners.

PARK AVENUE, SWEDESBORO, N. J.
Pub.A.M.Simon.324 E.23rd St.,N.Y.

Benjamin C. Clark, owner of Clark's Hotel, bought several building lots along Park Avenue in 1895 and built some of the first houses there. In August 1895, the street was officially opened from Lake Avenue down to the cemetery and a new bridge span was built crossing the Battentown branch of Church Run.

MILL STREET,
11979   Swedesboro, N. J.   Pub by Guest & Guest

Residents along Franklin Street today find the setting to be very tranquil, like the quiet street shown here in 1910. Franklin Street, also known as Mill Hill, became a favorite location for sledding during the wintertime. Jack Adams lived in a house at far left. The Swedesboro Agricultural Implement shop and the Titus machine shop at the corner of Lake Avenue and Franklin Street brought noise and traffic to the street while they existed.

This stately house in Woolwich Township is called Grand Sprute farm, named for the small tributary along the east boundary. The farm was once part of 500 acres bought jointly by the Swedish Morton and Archer families, who settled in West Jersey in 1695. This house was owned at the time of the Revolutionary War by George Van Leer. His son-in-law Samuel Black bought the home from the other Van Leer heirs, and the farm remained in the Black family until about 1912. (Courtesy GCHS.)

This brownstone farmhouse on Hendrickson Road was the family home of Isaac Hendrickson, who died in 1833 from an accident at the sawmill. Hendrick Hendrickson, by his will of 1749, left the farm property to his son Henry Hendrickson, who built the sawmill before 1772. The house and farm remained in the possession of Hendrickson's descendants until 1927.

RESIDENCE OF MR. AMOS HURFF.

Amos Hurff was a resident of Center Square while it was still part of Woolwich Township. He owned a large farm of about 120 acres. When he retired in 1895, he moved off the farm to this small castle at the corner of Grant Avenue. The house had an impressive tower room on both the second and third stories. The wraparound porch made Hurff's home a popular spot to chat on Main Street.

This large family has gathered to celebrate Decoration Day in Swedesboro. The tradition started locally in 1866, the year after the Civil War ended. The community gathered as one with a solemn procession beginning at the Methodist cemetery, where flowers were laid on the graves of soldiers who died during the war. After a few speeches, the group moved to the Episcopal cemetery, and then concluded the remembrance event at the Roman Catholic cemetery. Years later, Decoration Day became the federal holiday observed in May as Memorial Day.

Six

INDUSTRY GROWS

The New Star Car
The Big Sensation of the Year

Touring	$490
Roadster	$490
Sedan	$785
Coupe	$640
Special Touring	$640
Special Sedan	$935

f. o. b. Lansing, Mich.

A. C. DODD
SWEDESBORO, N. J.

The Star automobile was produced from 1922 to 1926 by the Durant Motor Company of Lansing, Michigan. There was also a Durant assembly plant in Elizabeth, New Jersey. In 1923, Durant added a station wagon model, the first of its kind in the United States. Swedesboro had a number of automobile dealerships, including Ford, Chevrolet, Chrysler, and the Hupmobile.

Constantine Damask started learning the candy business in the 1930s from his father, Nicholas Damask, an immigrant from Greece who had moved his candy business from Philadelphia to Swedesboro, where he opened a store on Main Street in 1921. Constantine and his wife, Martha, moved out to Woolwich Township to build their own candy store. Today, it is operated by their son Doug. (Courtesy Doug Damask.)

The Swedesboro Glass Works was organized in 1885, with local businessmen being the shareholders. It was sold in 1906 to a company based in Newark, New Jersey, and operated as the South Jersey Glass Works. After a disastrous fire in 1912, the plant was rebuilt as seen here and modernized with bottle blowing machines. From 1913 to 1918, it was owned by the Glenshaw Glass Company of Pennsylvania. The glassworks closed for good in 1923.

The Bottles shown here are from different eras of the Holly Springs Water Company. The bottle at right was hand-blown, produced at the Swedesboro Glass Works. The bottle second from left includes the name of Andrew J. Haas, who took over Holly Springs in 1906. By 1920, Joseph C. Powell was running the business. He later moved to Neptune, Florida, and took his soda bottling business with him.

Food processing at Hurff's canning factory continued into autumn, long after the end of the tomato harvest. Here, workers are unloading a wagon of pumpkins. The pumpkins would be split in half and the seeds scooped out and saved for the next planting. The factory started in April, as soon as asparagus was ready. In the late spring, asparagus was followed by green beans. (Courtesy New Jersey State Archives; Department of State.)

Before there was a canning plant, Edgar Hurff ran a seed supply business. Once the canning plant opened, there was an endless supply of seeds. Here, workers behind the factory are washing tomato seeds to be processed. The factory buildings and all equipment were sold to the Del Monte Corporation in 1948. (Courtesy New Jersey State Archives; Department of State.)

When Edgar Hurff began his canning business in 1913, he found a site on Water Street with access to regional transportation. Hurff believed the railroad would help minimize his transportation costs. During World War II, a young soldier from Swedesboro wrote home to tell his father, one of Hurff's cooks, that he had found a piece of home in the South Pacific, as Hurff's tomato juice had been served at his dinner meal. (Courtesy GCHS.)

74

William W. Dilks was already a successful operator of a lumberyard in Pitman in 1916, when he saw an opportunity for producing wooden baskets and crates in Swedesboro. He purchased one acre of land from Helen Richardson along the railroad tracks and started a basket factory from the ground up. Dilks's factory had a number of modern machines, and began turning out farm packages by September 1916. (Courtesy New Jersey State Archives; Department of State.)

Three of the employees of W.W. Dilks and Son are shown here manufacturing climax baskets for packing fancy tomatoes. The baskets have multiple pieces of wood, which were stapled together. The basket bottom is the strongest, while the rim is also firmly held together. For packing baskets, a twist of wire was added to the top rim, and an independent lid was used to cover and protect the vegetables. (Courtesy New Jersey State Archives; Department of State.)

WM. J. BLACK,

Carriage and Wagon Builder,

Swedesboro, N. J.

Shops at South Swedesboro.

William J. Black was a craftsman and a wagon builder. In 1895, he started his own business in South Swedesboro, at the sheds along Mechanic Street. Black's skills were called on by the West Jersey and Seashore Railroad. He took a full-time job with the railroad and moved his family to Camden and then to Newark, New Jersey. They never returned to Swedesboro. William's sons Charles and George also found work as railroad firemen.

John C. Helms was a simple farmer in Bridgeport but left that sleepy town about 1890. He opened a meats and poultry business on Main Street. Business was so good that by 1902, Helms was an investor with the Lakeside Land Company. He also bought one of the lots and built the fine home at the corner of East Avenue and Main Street.

William Rode began in the poultry business in 1880. He started working out of a small building on his own farm and was soon taking chickens to market at a vendor's stall in Philadelphia. In time, his business grew from a small family concern; in 1916, it was passed to William's son Otto C. Rode and renamed. Today, Otto C. Rode Inc. is led by David Rode, William's great-great grandson

This liquor bottle bears the name of Harminus Madara, who manufactured his own beer and porter ale from a location in Battentown prior to 1870. This dark green bottle is extremely rare. It is handblown, but its age predates the period of operation of the Swedesboro Glass Works.

In 1925, Frank Schoener purchased the old blacksmith shop on Main Street and built a new automobile service garage. Initially, his business line was limited to vehicle battery sales. In time, Schoener's became a full-service garage with fuel pumps for Esso gasoline.

Arthur A. Hunter started one of the early transportation companies in Swedesboro, around 1920. He began with a few trucks, such as the one here, which hauled finished products for the Hurff company. Hunter expanded his services to include busses, which ran on regular routes to Camden from a depot located on the lot now occupied by the Woolwich Fire Hall.

This is one of Arthur A. Hunter's covered trucks for hauling just about any type of freight. The Hunter company worked out of a small property located between Main Street and Auburn Avenue. Hunter ran a trucking business from 1920 to 1928.

As a side venture to the trucking business, Arthur A. Hunter started up a passenger bus service, making daily trips between Swedesboro and Salem and traveling up to Camden. The busses were also popular for daylong charter trips, sometimes going to the seashore and sometimes to the Pocono Mountains. This photograph from 1922 shows a day tour that went to northeastern Pennsylvania.

George R. Hamilton was the local pharmacist in the late 1870s. He was also a manufacturer and distributor of patent medicines. On the reverse side of this card is an advertisement for Hamilton's Toothache Drops. This picture of Thomas A. Hendricks may be described as political campaign memorabilia. Hendricks was an 1876 vice presidential nominee. In 1884, Grover Cleveland was elected as president and Hendricks as vice president.

In 1920, Charles White bought the store of Guest and Guest and continued to provide pharmaceuticals to the residents of Swedesboro. White died about 1937, and his wife was no longer interested in the pharmacy. She sold that part of the business to John and Saul Ross, who relocated, with a new business name as the Lawall Pharmacy. (Courtesy GCHS.)

Seven

VIEW FROM THE WATER

Raccoon Creek, a tributary of the Delaware River, flows through the center of Woolwich Township and was the main route of travel and commerce until the railroad was built in 1869. The creek meanders for 12 miles through very fertile land. Approaching the town of Swedesboro, a traveler can see the Trinity Church steeple.

In the 1800s, the highly productive large farms were the center of an agricultural economy. The sandy soil, while ideal for growing vegetables and grains, needed fertilizers that were delivered by boats on the creek. Raising "truck" was the principal business. Products were shipped by sloops, barges, and later steamboats to Philadelphia and New York.

Landowners added to the natural vegetation by planting trees. The banks of the freshwater tidal marshes were covered with nine-foot-tall wild rice plants, which fed flocks of migrating birds. Broad-leafed cattails and water hemp abounded. Bald eagles nested near the waterway, and beautiful colored sunflowers added to the scenery.

The stately Federal-style house located on the corner of Kings Highway and Glen Echo Avenue was built by David Harker, a wealthy merchant and landowner, in 1784 and purchased by George A. Rode in 1902. Rode managed his father William Rode's ice, coal, and manure business. The back of the house faced Raccoon Creek, which at that time was a navigable tributary of the Delaware River.

Lotus Lilies (Nelumbium Luteum).

From a photo by E. W. Humphreys, Publisher, Woodstown, N. J. These rare and showy lilies grow in profusion in the pond at Sharptown, near Woodstown, N. J., blooming in July. Supposed to have been introduced here by the Indians, who are said to have used the roots and seeds as food. The flowers, some of which stand five feet out of water, measure from five to ten inches across, and some of the leaves are over two feet in diameter.

Local ponds and marshes such as the Glen Echo Spring and creek areas were resplendent in the springtime with blooming lotus lilies. The giant leaves of the plants are as beautiful as the white and pale-yellow flowers. Among the plants, aquatic birds such as the great heron fed. Indians used parts of the plants as food; the edible seeds are known as "alligator corn."

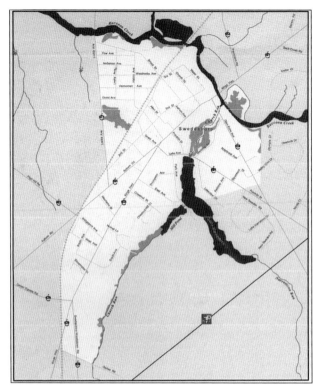

In 2012, an Environmental Resource Inventory was conducted by the Delaware Valley Regional Planning Commission for Swedesboro. The study was "to unite the region's elected officials, planning professionals and the public with a common vision of making a great region greater." Among the inventoried items are maps of local waterways. Map 11 of Appendix G depicts Raccoon Creek, Church Run, Lake Narraticon, and Mill Pond. (Courtesy DVRPC report.)

The flood of 1940 caused much damage to the area when the banks of Raccoon Creek overflowed due to the dam at Lake Narraticon bursting. The Kings Highway bridge, Rodeville homes on Paulsboro Road, and Al Caltabiano's and Retino's service stations were inundated with about five feet of water. Pictured is the new Atlantic station at the corner of Kings Highway and Paulsboro Road surrounded with water.

Lake Narraticon, Swedesboro, N. J.

Lake Narraticon was formed when a dam was built across Church Run, a stream that ran east from Raccoon Creek toward Lake Park Cemetery. The name of the waterway refers to the fact that Trinity Church owned most of the property along the stream. Beyond the bridge and the dam, a mill can be seen. Waterpower from the dam created a perfect location for the many mills around the lake.

ROAD AND VIEW OF LAKE, SWEDESBORO, N. J.

A later view showing telephone poles includes more houses and the dam between Church Run and the lake. The many businesses on both sides of the lake, which milled grist, plaster, woolens, and wood, depended on waterpower. The mill tracts played a large part in the development of Swedesboro. Later, as the mills diminished, the town gained homes and businesses.

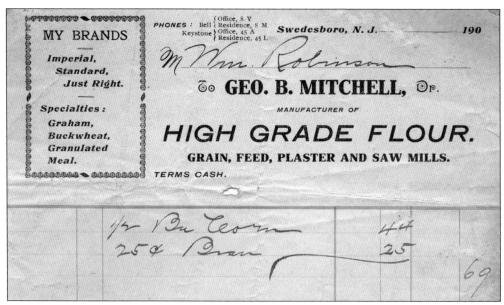

In the mid-1800s, farming and milling were becoming the economic engine for Swedesboro and Woolwich Township. The fertile soil and natural woodlands provided materials for the many mills. George Batten Mitchell, a mill owner, was a manufacturer and dealer in flour, grain, plaster, and lumber. He was regarded as one of Swedesboro's most energetic and successful businessmen. His gristmill was on Church Run and Mill Street, now known as Franklin Street.

Not all mills were located around Lake Narraticon. Surrounding mills were situated on local waterways. Oliphant's mill was on Oldman's Creek near Sharptown Road. Warrington's was on Purgey Branch on the road from Bridgeport. Vanderbilt's mill had five owners before John Vanderbilt bought the property. The mill was located in Woolwich Township near the county line. Mills were categorized by "runs of stones" to determine the grade of the grain.

A pumping station on Franklin Street at the lake was needed to direct town water. In July 1934, water pressure from heavy rains caused the dam and bridge to collapse. The building pictured was undermined, along with the backyards of surrounding properties. The sight of a somewhat dry lake was eerie. Soon after, several property owners sought damages from the borough. Mrs. George Rode's barn was wrecked, and Antone Frederick's Mill Street garage was washed away. The pumping station equipment was buried under several feet of water, and the mud damaged motors and machinery.

Glen Echo,
Swedesboro, N. J.

Glen Echo Spring must have been a popular place to visit because of the number of existing postcards. J. Jenning's farm was located off the North Branch of Raccoon Creek. The 1876 Woolwich Township map shows the location of the property between Glen Echo Avenue and the creek. A bridge and pathway provided access to the spring and fishing pond.

A spring water company named Holly Springs was located on the old Jennings farm in the early 1900s. In later years, this property was the home of Walter Hunter. To attract Philadelphia summer visitors, the Jennings brothers began to bottle water from the spring. The ownership changed hands several times. Later bottles show the name of Joseph C. Powell. Subsequently, water was replaced by soda water.

Shipping local produce and lumber was an important industry in the area of Swedesboro and Woolwich from the early settlement years. Produce and timber were hauled by horse-drawn wagons to the wharves along Raccoon Creek to be shipped to Philadelphia, New York City, and Wilmington. Return shipments of manufactured products, such as milled lumber for construction, were essential. In the 1800s, the creek was narrower and deeper. Stratton's, the main wharf, was located opposite the tollgate on Kings Highway and Paulsboro Road. There was another wharf that was accessed by a road through the Trinity Church cemetery.

By World War II, water traffic on Raccoon Creek was limited to the transportation of fertilizer. In the spring, the Bridgeport Wright Brothers' two boats made weekly trips to the Royster Fertilizer Company in Baltimore, Maryland, to pick up fertilizer and deliver it to their warehouse in Swedesboro to be sold by Casella Brothers. The trip took almost 10 hours—two hours of which were up Raccoon Creek. Wright Brothers ceased operations in the late 1960s.

Early vessels were sloops and steamboats. In 1833–1834, John Burk purchased a small sloop, the *Hornet*, to ship produce. He expanded his business to more trips and began to carry passengers. In 1835, the Steamboat Company was organized. The larger vessels could carry greater loads of produce. After the Civil War, water carriage declined; in 1869, the introduction of the railroad in Swedesboro curtailed the significant water transportation. Commerce did continue, but with smaller vessels.

Eight

FAMILIAR PUBLIC BUILDINGS

Shown in this 1915 card, the newly opened municipal building was a two-story structure of Colonial Revival architecture designed by Simon and Bassett of Philadelphia. Included was a clock tower, which was paid for by public subscription and fundraising events. Refurbished in 2007, the clock is now electrically wound. The second-floor balcony (not shown here) was added later.

Police Chief Ted Damask is crossing kindergarten and first-grade students led by teacher Marcia West from the Auburn Avenue School after their visit to the Swedesboro Public Library for story time. The new firehouse was not built until around 1973. The bell, which was moved there, is still at this older location. Black drapes indicate a fireman had died. Note the telephone booth at right. (Courtesy J. Damask.)

In 1902, the Borough of Swedesboro assumed control of the fire department. The building pictured was the first city hall and fire department and was located on the site of the current building. A bell had been needed since the late 1800s, when the Trinity Church bell was used to alert the department of a fire. In April 1917, a fire tower was erected to hold a newly purchased bell.

The original location of the borough hall and the fire company was on the corner of Lake Avenue and Main Street, behind Hewes Black's cooperative building, shown on the right. The first floor housed stores and a Masonic hall upstairs. After 1915, the post office was located here. The building stood until it was demolished in 1972.

MAIN STREET, SWEDESBORO, N. J.

Borough Hall
Swedesboro, N. J.

24768

Wide, arched doors provided an entrance for the fire engines and a large interior room to hold apparatus. The first floor included a steel cell room and sanitary arrangements. A wide hallway and oak stairs led to the mayor's and clerk's offices. A very modern touch was a folded door wall, which could be arranged to make two rooms or one large meeting room. The current first-floor offices were added during a later renovation.

BOROUGH HALL, SWEDESBORO, N. J.

This view of the borough hall looking north toward Main Street shows the added balcony constructed to oversee public events. The Black Building, which was later demolished, is shown with an overhanging roof. In this pre–air conditioned era, many local businesses had such roofs to shade shoppers and keep stores cool. Of interest is the hitching post seen next to the fire hydrant.

A news article reporting on the dedication of the borough hall and housing of motorized fire apparatus in 1916 cited the affair as "the greatest day in Swedesboro's history." The parade included many neighboring fire departments. Special music was supplied by local bands and Mummers groups. Dedicated that day was the Waterous engine, a combination engine and hose cart costing $5,750. Prizes were awarded to fire companies and to local decorated residences.

Frank "Pop" Netherby was Swedesboro's beloved school crossing guard at the Auburn Avenue School. He annually played Santa Claus to the schoolchildren and, like Santa, made wooden gifts. The painted and decaled wooden stools and clothes trees are still treasured. Unable to make presents one year, he presented each child with a copy of this photograph. (Courtesy C. Dupper, D. Gage.)

A homecoming and dedication ceremony was held on November 11, 1946. At this time, a wooden Roll of Honor plaque listing the names of those who served in World Wars I and II was unveiled by Frances S. Timmins, whose brother Herbert Sparks was killed in action. The plaque was paid for by the area service clubs. Rev. Parker F. Auten gave the invocation, and Mayor Lawrence L. Crispin welcomed the crowd. At the close of the program, the group marched to Swedesboro Lake to dedicate a community bathhouse.

Many area students attended school at this beautiful Romanesque Revival gray stone building. The beautiful front and rear Palladian windows and stone arch lintels are outstanding. One-room country schools, named for locations such as Battentown and Oak Grove, still existed in 1909 when this building was constructed. Students attended the high school for ninth and tenth grades.

Built in 1909 on Kings Highway, this stately structure was named Swedesboro High School, for grades kindergarten through 10. At the end of 10th grade, students chose to attend Woodstown or Woodbury High Schools. Travel to these schools was by train or by a newly established bus route. This early postcard shows a completed building and incomplete landscaping.

In the late 1900s, an iron fence was added to the school property to enclose the play yard. The planting of oak trees to shade the three-story stone building completed the landscaping. Due to disrepair, the fence was removed recently and replaced with low cement curbing and landscaping.

In the early 1960s, the gray stone building was purchased from the local board of education by the Catholic diocese for a school for grades kindergarten through eight. The sale was part of a reorganization of the public schools when Kingsway Regional High School was built. Previously, St. Joseph's parochial school held classes in the old Catholic church seen here, which had been moved to the back of the church property.

Swedesboro High School was open from 1923 to 1963 as a secondary school and educated students from Swedesboro, Woolwich, and East Greenwich. The brick Colonial-style building cost $233,000 fully furnished. According to the county superintendent at the time, Swedesboro had the costliest school in the county. The building currently houses grade six of the Swedesboro-Woolwich District.

Shown here in a freshman class photograph is the Swedesboro High School class of 1935. Class officers for the year were Ellison Haines, president; Jane O'Connor, vice president; Samuel Patterson, secretary; and Othniel Merion, treasurer. Among the other members pictured are Gladys Gaines, Robert Hendrickson, Kenneth Horner, Peter Musumeci, Inez Reymer, Betty Rode, Sidney Rode, George Schoener, and Margaret Seehousz. Advisors were Isabel Sager and Joe Bona.

In 1942, Edger Hurff donated the previous Swedesboro Trust Company building to the Borough of Swedesboro to be used as a public library. Now part of the Gloucester County Library System, the Swedesboro Library was established in 1783 and incorporated in 1937, making it one of the oldest libraries in New Jersey. The current neoclassical marble building built around 1913 replaced a stone residence with attached post office.

The US Post Office Department began issuing pre-stamped postal cards in 1873 as an easy way to send short notes. Before the current Swedesboro Trust Company was built, postmaster James J. Davidson built a gray stone home and post office. In 1893, the spelling of Swedesborough was changed to Swedesboro. When his house was torn down to make way for the bank, Davidson built a brownstone house next door, which is still a private residence.

Woolwich Township was named for the town of Woolwich, located on the river Thames in England and noted for its large arsenal. Reportedly, the first township building was on Kings Highway just over the Raccoon Creek Bridge. In 1937, a new building was constructed on Woodstown Road south of Swedesboro. The plot was purchased from Samuel W. Ogden for $500. Mayor Mayhew Davidson was joined by a committee of five men to govern. The township hall was used by the Swedesboro Grange for meetings, elections, dinners, and parties. The Second Saturday Night Club hosted by Stoney Harris, owner of Cowtown Rodeo, held social affairs here. Subsequently, the building became the Woolwich Township Municipal Building, which was used until the new building on Center Square Road was built. (Both, courtesy Woolwich Township.)

Nine

TIME FOR REFLECTION

The First Presbyterian Church of Swedesboro
was built in 1855. The year before, the
congregation was incorporated at a
meeting held in the Swedesboro Academy.
It elected as trustees William Black Jr.,
Robert Wilson, Hugh Wallace, J. Morgan
Barnes, and Ira Allen. In 1873, an influx of
German immigrants added to the number
of worshipers. Most of these had affiliated
with the German Reformed Church in the
old country.

In this early 1900s postcard, the small, simple, frame St Joseph's Roman Catholic Church is shown with the rectory next to it. The origin of this church goes back to the 1840s, when many Irish immigrants held services in private homes. After much planning, a new building was dedicated in 1861. By 1898, a much-needed new rectory was built, and the one pictured was constructed. It has been demolished in recent years.

The second St. Joseph's Church, now St. Clare of Assisi, was built in 1925 and basically remains the same. The Tudor Gothic–style structure was of limestone and granite. The Catholic church has contributed to the community over the years. The Feast of St. Alfio is a tribute to the Sicilian roots of the Italian farmers. In the 1970s, a need arose to address the many Hispanic church members. Masses in Spanish were added.

The Bethesda Methodist Church was built in 1886 near the corner of Main Street and Railroad Avenue. The two-story brick structure replaced the original church built in 1838. The new building was actually constructed with the old structure inside. The parsonage is shown to the right of the church in this picture.

In Methodist churches, a Rally Day was held in early September to renew effort to involve children and their teachers in the Sunday school classes for Christian education. All children would attend a worship service, be assigned teachers and classrooms, and then attend a luncheon. The handwritten note on this 1912 postcard is from Thomas S. Hammond, who was minister of Bethesda Methodist Church in Swedesboro from 1912 to 1915.

Old Stone Meeting House near Swedesboro, New Jersey

In 1793, Joseph and Elizabeth Adams deeded one acre of land to Francis Asbury and Thomas Coke, superintendents of the Methodist Episcopal Church. The intersection of Stone Meeting House and Oak Grove Roads was a convenient place for a church. About halfway between Swedesboro and Bridgeport was handy for churchgoers to attend by paddling across Raccoon Creek and walking the rest of the way. Adjoining the church is a graveyard enclosed by a stone wall. Names such as Adams, Daniels, Fish, and Horner can be seen on markers—some as early as the 1800s. In 1987, the deteriorating condition caused the brownstone building to be closed. The Friends of Old Stone—Charles Homan, J. Marvin Dare, Jack Wright, George Shiveler, and Russell Shiveler—undertook a restoration project. In 1993, the renovated church was dedicated in celebration of its 200th anniversary.

ZION CHAPEL, MORAVIA (1786)
Old Moravian Church, Sharptown Road at Oldman's Creek *N.J.*

The Moravian church is located on the Swedesboro Sharptown Road about three miles south of Swedesboro. Dissenters from the Trinity Episcopal Church in Swedesboro established the Zion Moravian Church of Oldman's Creek in 1743. The present brick building was dedicated in 1786. This W.W. Humphrey's card depicts the fenced building and a covered side entrance. The original altar was once used in Trinity Church in Swedesboro. After the decline of Moravian membership, Methodists and Episcopalians worshipped here. Beginning in 1838, the property belonged to the Protestant Episcopal Church of New Jersey. Since 1948, it has been owned by the Gloucester Country Historical Society and is currently being renovated.

Moravian Church, near Swedesboro, New Jersey. Dedicated 1786.

The Swedish Lutheran Church at Raccoon met in a log cabin structure prior to the Revolutionary War. In 1778, the Redcoats marched through Swedesboro on the way to a skirmish at Hancock's Bridge. The old church was so badly despoiled by both the British and Colonial militia units that rector Nicholas Collin began a new building campaign in 1783. This fine Georgian-style structure was completed in 1784.

Pictured in the early 1930s, Trinity Church presents an imposing structure as one enters Swedesboro. The building on the left is the Lippincott Gaskill hardware store, now Trinity Square. The horse sheds visible behind the church were torn down, and the ground became available for newer burials. By this time, houses had been built on Water Street, as seen to the right in this card.

108

The interior of Trinity Church has gone through many renovations. To replace the original center aisle seating arrangement, the two side aisles with boxed seats were installed in 1830. At one time, the interior was painted in the decorative Classical Revival style, and in the 1960s the decor returned to the more plain Colonial Revival to be more authentic. Lighting was improved over the years from candles to gas and electric fixtures.

The venetian blinds purchased in 1837 can be seen in this 1900 photograph of the interior of Trinity Church. Records show that they have been repaired over the years. Electricity and light fixtures were installed in 1890. The altar rail does not have an opening, and classical stenciling is seen above the altar. The pipe organ located on the first floor is seen to the right.

CHURCH STREET.
11977   Swedesboro, N.J.

Pub by
Guest & Guest

Showing the back side of Trinity Church in a view looking toward Kings Highway, this early card includes a low, wooden post fence along the cemetery. The house of Samuel Guest can be seen in the distance, and what is now Trinity Square is to the right. The five-story tower, modeled after the Independence Hall tower in Philadelphia, was added in 1838. Church Street was paved in the early 1900s.

Trinity Church's exterior has not changed over the years. Kings Highway was paved in 1936. Milestones of Swedish settlement have been celebrated by festivities—the centennial in 1884, the bicentennial in 1902, the tercentenary in 1938, and the nation's bicentennial in 1976. Swedish royalty have visited the church, including Prince Bertil in 1938 and King Carl XVI Gustaf in 1976. The church was listed in National Register of Historic Places in 1971.

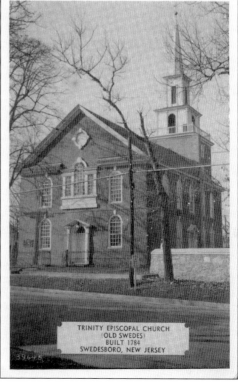

TRINITY EPISCOPAL CHURCH
(OLD SWEDES)
BUILT 1784
SWEDESBORO, NEW JERSEY

In 1938, Swedish crown prince Gustaf Adolf was to visit Swedesboro, but when he fell ill, his brother Prince Bertil visited Trinity Church on the occasion of the tercentenary celebration of the arrival of the Swedes on the Delaware. A plaque commemorating the settlement was dedicated. The plaque is still on the rear interior wall of the church. Seen here are Rev. Joseph Urban, Prince Bertil, and an unidentified state trooper.

On April 8, 1976, King Carl XVI Gustaf of Sweden arrived in Swedesboro to dedicate a memorial in front of Trinity Church. The king was greeted by Rev. Parker F. Auten, Gov. Brendan Byrne, Swedesboro mayor Luciano Vasta, and Woolwich mayor Albert Stecher. The occasion was to commemorate Sweden's part in the settlement of the area and was part of the American bicentennial celebration.

Hymn

A Mighty fortress is our God,
A bulwark never failing;
Our helper he amid the flood
Of mortal ills prevailing:
For still our ancient foe
Doth seek to work us woe;
His craft and power are great,
And, armed with cruel hate,
On earth is not his equal.

Did we in our own strength confide,
Our striving would be losing;
Were not the right man on our side,
The man of God's own choosing:
Dost ask who that may be?
Christ Jesus, it is he;
Lord Sabaoth his Name,
From age to age the same,
And he must win the battle.

MARTIN LUTHER, 1529

Points of   Interest

INSIDE THE CHURCH:
* Swedish Bible presented personally by King Gustav V of Sweden, grandfather of the present King.
* The Swedish Flag.
* The Memorial Tablet on the back wall.
* Two old oil lamps in the front windows.
* The very old venetian blinds.
* Door weight consisting of a stone in a leather bag.
* The old pews and hardware.
* Picture of the old Silver Communion Service.

OUTSIDE:
* Monument in New Sweden Park marking the site of the log Church, 1703.
* Bicentennial monument commemorating the visit of His Majesty Carl XVI Gustaf, King of Sweden, 1976.
* Historical plaque on the outside wall of the Church.
* The Parish House on Kings Highway at the foot of Church Street, built in 1854.
* The Rectory at 208 Kings Highway, built in 1865 on the site of the first Rectory, built in 1765.

A Program to Celebrate the Visit
of
His Majesty Carl XVI Gustaf,
King of Sweden

TRINITY (OLD SWEDES) CHURCH, SWEDESBORO, NEW JERSEY

APRIL 8, 1976

Completing a large project, iron gates were installed at the entrance to the Trinity Church Cemetery in 1862. Many notable persons are interred in the graveyard. Among them are Dr. Bodo Otto Jr., who was Gen. George Washington's physician at Valley Forge; Col. Thomas Heston, who revitalized the Stanger glassworks of Glassboro; and Eric Mullica, whose sons founded Mullica Hill. The Mortenson/Schorn log cabin is located in the churchyard. (Courtesy Swedesboro Economic Development.)

The "New" Trinity Cemetery, located two blocks from the church, was purchased around 1812. Thirty Civil War veterans as well as prominent local residents are interred at this resting place. Gen. Louis Henry Carpenter, a Medal of Honor recipient, is one. His troops were called buffalo soldiers during his service in the Indian Territory. Charles Creighton Stratton, the first popularly elected governor of New Jersey, is also buried here. (Courtesy Swedesboro Economic Development.)

Lake, Swedesboro, N. J.

The early photograph of Cemetery Drive at right shows the larger Lake Narraticon on the right and the Mill Pond, known as the "little lake," on the left. In the 1907 card above, a clearer view of the Mill Pond shows its relationship to the larger body of water. Over the years, Cemetery Drive was improved by road surfacing and bridge construction. Lake Park Cemetery was financed by a few wealthy borough businessmen. In *Swedesboro Yesterday and Today*, Mayor Wilmer Egee speaks of the cemetery as "a beautiful spot lying south west of the town on the banks of a pretty little lake which washes two sides of it."

At Lake Park Cemetery in 2000, the Swedesboro-Woolwich Historical Society and the 12th New Jersey Infantry honored Civil War captain Charles D. Lippincott by presenting his sword to the Swedesboro Library. Often wounded, Lippincott participated in almost all of the 12th New Jersey's skirmishes. After his service career, he was a partner in the Lippincott and Gaskill hardware store for 37 years.

Henry C. Garrison is buried in Lake Park Cemetery. After limited service in the Civil War, he returned to his native home in 1864 and was elected collector and constable of Woolwich Township. As county sheriff, deputy, and detective, he arrested many horse thieves. From 1897 to 1906, he served as a US deputy marshal.

Ten

TIME FOR FUN

The Swedesboro Ball Club field was located on vacant land between Glen Echo Avenue and Franklin Street. The entrance to the field was on Merkling Street. According to an article in the *Woodbury Constitution* on October 17, 1914, Connie Mack's Philadelphia Athletics played the local team. Over 3,000 people attended the popular event. The A's won by a score of 9-2. The paper reported that "it was a friendly game and everyone was pleased."

The Swedesboro AC baseball team defeated the Woodbury Police nine to earn the title of champions in 1949. Manager Cleveland "Jake" Sholders's players were from Swedesboro and the surrounding area. The celebration festivities were held at the American Legion field on Franklin Street. In 1949, Swedesboro High School's baseball team, the Little Swedes, and the East Greenwich Mohawks all won titles.

Recreational activities on Swedesboro Lake have always been popular. A 1906 postcard notes the lake "is a good place for canoeing." Row boating, swimming, and fishing were common activities. The 200-acre "hidden gem" at the end of East and Park Avenues has provided enjoyment for generations of residents. Through the years, Scouting activities, family reunions, Red Cross swimming lessons, and trail hiking have been popular.

COPYRIGHT BY A. S. JOHNSON JR.

ENOUGH FOR DINNER

In his "How We Do Things" series, early photographer Alfred Stanley Johnson exaggerates the size of fish caught in local waterways. Lake Narraticon is home to several species of fish. Among them are bass, pickerel, catfish, perch, carp, and sunfish. In recent years, the lake has been stocked with trout, much to the delight of fishermen. The 1940s "Greeting from Swedesboro" card below is a more realistic depiction of a favorite pastime for young boys. Their rolled-up dungarees, homemade fishing poles, and tin can bait containers are reminiscent of a simpler boyhood diversion— perhaps reminding the recipient of Tom Sawyer and Huckleberry Finn.

GREETINGS FROM SWEDESBORO, N. J.   L-109

17,354

EMBASSY
THEATRE · SWEDESBORO

WEDNESDAY EVENING JULY 22   2 - GOOD FEATURES
VICTOR McLAGLEN & EDMUND LOWE in
CALL OUT THE MARINES
and ZANE GREY'S
LONE STAR RANGER
JOHN KIMBROUGH & SHEILA RYAN
SATURDAY MAT. & EVE. JULY 25   2 GREAT HITS
JOE E. BROWN
SHUT MY BIG MOUTH
AND WILLIAM LUNDIGAN & SHIRLEY ROSS
SAILORS ON LEAVE
WEDNESDAY EVE. JULY 29
RED SKELTON - ELEANOR POWELL
"SHIP AHOY"
with TOMMY DORSEY & ORCHESTRA
SATURDAY MAT. & EVE. AUG. 1   2 ★ SWELL SHOWS ★ 2
RICHARD ARLEN & JEAN PARKER in
TORPEDO BOAT
and ROY ROGERS in
ROMANCE ON THE RANGE

Swimming in Lake Narraticon has been popular over the years. Homeowners along the lake had private docks from which to boat and swim. In 1942, a public bathhouse, paid for by local businesses, was dedicated to the community. This is a 1920 photograph from the Hunter family album. Jack Hunter is sitting in the water closest to the camera; Violet and Jessie Penn are a little further out.

The Embassy Theater closed in 1950. Opening in 1915 as Shoemaker's Opera House on Allen Street, the location is now part of Botto's parking lot. The playhouse seated 400 people and hosted operas, movies, and vaudeville. The original building became Shoemaker's Garage as well as housing the theater. The entire complex was demolished in 1961.

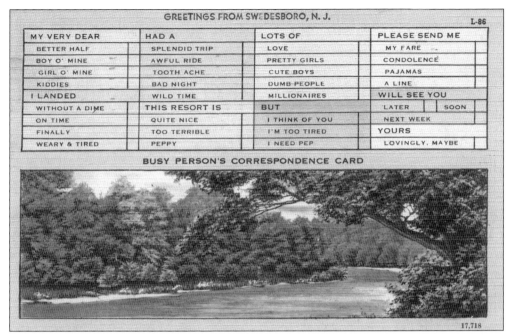

GREETINGS FROM SWEDESBORO, N. J.

L-86

MY VERY DEAR	HAD A	LOTS OF	PLEASE SEND ME	
BETTER HALF	SPLENDID TRIP	LOVE	MY FARE	
BOY O' MINE	AWFUL RIDE	PRETTY GIRLS	CONDOLENCE	
GIRL O' MINE	TOOTH ACHE	CUTE BOYS	PAJAMAS	
KIDDIES	BAD NIGHT	DUMB PEOPLE	A LINE	
I LANDED	WILD TIME	MILLIONAIRES	WILL SEE YOU	
WITHOUT A DIME	THIS RESORT IS	BUT	LATER	SOON
ON TIME	QUITE NICE	I THINK OF YOU	NEXT WEEK	
FINALLY	TOO TERRIBLE	I'M TOO TIRED	YOURS	
WEARY & TIRED	PEPPY	I NEED PEP	LOVINGLY, MAYBE	

BUSY PERSON'S CORRESPONDENCE CARD

17,718

Sometimes straightforward and sometimes humorous, the Busy Person's Correspondence Card was popular in the 1940s–1950s. The multicolored, boxed-style cards were designed to save the time and trouble of writing longer notes. Vacation themes such as beach excursions, fishing trips, and city visits were frequent topics. Outhouse humor was a less popular subject. The generic photograph of the lake here seems to suggest Lake Narraticon.

Sometimes, postcards made social commentary in an exaggerated, humorous manner. In the early 1900s, Alfred Stanley Johnson, a photographer from Waupun, Wisconsin, published several series of cards. These depictions of turn-of-the-century rural life became known as tall-tale postcards. Published in 1915, Joy Ride, from the "Scene on the Road" series, comments on the undependability of the motorcar vs. the older horse and buggy mode of transportation.

Gruppo Della Societa Independente
Italo-Americana Catania
In Occasione Battesimo Bandiere
Sept. 20, 1939
Swedesboro, N. J.

The Catania Society, an offshoot of the Gloria Dei Society, was formed after a rift between members of the original organization. The Societa Independente Italo-Americana Catania was named after a province in the members' ancestral homeland, Sicily. Pictured is the flag christening held on September 20, 1939. Both groups fostered strong kinship and were mutual

aid organizations with educational, cultural, and beneficiary purposes. At their house at 100 Kings Highway, meetings as well as social events, such as dinners and weddings, were held. Membership was male, with women organizing special occasions. Leadership was recognized by special sashes. Both organizations held religious processions to honor St. Joseph and St. Alfio.

Local members of the Crescent Shriners Temple are pictured at a convention in Atlantic City. The temple was founded in 1904 and was a Fraternal Organization of Master Masons. Their purpose was fun, fellowship, and pursuing brotherly love, relief, and truth. The fez was a recognizable symbol. Ulysses Sherman Estilow, second from left in the back row, was a much-respected businessman of Swedesboro. The Shriners are well known for their children's hospital support.

Among local residents attending a Shriners' convention in Atlantic City in 1925 are members of the Hunter, Rainey, Horneff, Shreiber, and Williamson families. Arthur A. Hunter (standing on the left) was mayor of Swedesboro from 1926 to 1929 and was responsible for lowering the fire insurance rate, suggesting new water mains, purchasing new fire apparatus, and instituting a building code.

Harold S. Twiss, Secretary

I will attend the Eighth and Final Meeting of the

Sunday Morning Breakfast Club April 27th, 1952.

W. V. Molitor

Signed _____

The Swedesboro Sunday Morning Breakfast Club started in 1942 when some Trinity Church members met and talked of their concern of the war and the Swedesboro area boys leaving to fight. Soon after, the Kiwanians joined the breakfast group, and it became a nondenominational organization. Members were notified by postcard to determine attendance. Early member names included Kirchhoff, Nothdurft, Rode, Crispin, Hunter, Homan, Netherby, Shiveler and Peterson.

Jean Haines, Lena Hunter, Florence Hunter, and Doris Fitzgerald Lucas, members of the Kingsway Riding Club, are pictured in this 1940 photograph taken at the Gloucester County Horse Show. The show was sponsored by the Bit and Bridle Club of Wenonah and was held at the Camden Airport. The Kingsway Club was active from 1938 to 1940.

Excursions to the New Jersey beaches were common. Often, young people went on day trip dates to bathe in the ocean or to just sit and enjoy the scenery. This 1911 photograph of John A. Adams Sr. and friends was taken just before Wildwood became a city. The Wildwood and Delaware Bay Shore Line Railroad had just been completed. The Reading Railroad Line trains ran to Wildwood often. In 1912, the Atlantic City boardwalk was adopted as a model for Wildwood's pier and amusement rides.

Perhaps the postcard was America's first form of social media. Actual studio family photographs were the forerunners of today's family Christmas photographic cards. Often, the card included a baby or toddler, many times posed in a coach or on a wagon. Pictured in this 1910 card are Ida Molitor and her children Walter, Arthur, and Marian. The photograph was taken at Lipp Studios in Philadelphia. (Courtesy L. Stanley.)

Greeting cards were popularized in the United States in the 1880s, when offset lithography made them inexpensive. By the 1900s, in order to entice customers into buying more postcards, tinsel or glittered cards were sold. These German-made "Welcome To," "Greetings From," or "Happy Birthday" cards were popular. Because the glitter rubbed off on postal clerks' hands, the cards were deemed hazardous and had to be mailed in envelopes.

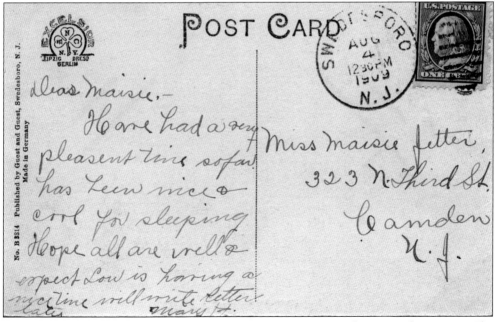

Prior to the telephone, postcards were used to communicate simple, practical messages. The weather, health issues, relatives seen, or travel arrangements were common topics. This August 1909 Guest and Guest card from Mary to her friend Maisie is just such a missive. Guest and Guest, a local pharmacy, published German-made cards. Mail service, often two deliveries each day, enabled residents to send quick messages.

Of all holiday postcards, Christmas greetings were the most popular. Printer Louis Prang, a Prussian immigrant, introduced the Christmas card to America in 1875. His first cards were of flowers with the simple message "Merry Christmas." Later cards elicited homey emotions by depicting snowy rural farmhouses and churches. Other popular images were poinsettias, holly, and bells. The card pictured was sent from Utica, New York, to Swedesboro in 1907.

Pennant postcards were called stock cards, which were printed with just a standard greeting, no text, and a generic image. Sometimes, the image was not exactly appropriate, as is the case with this Dutch boy. A Swedish child would have been more suitable for Swedesboro. A local store with an inexpensive hand press could insert the hometown name.

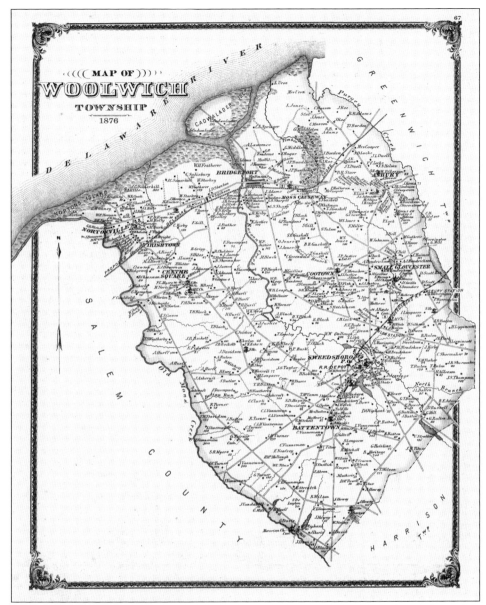

This map of Woolwich Township shows how densely it was settled by 1876. The total area shown is 50 square miles, or 32,000 acres. Shortly after this map was made, a new township was set off in 1877. Originally called West Woolwich Township, it was renamed Logan Township a year later. Woolwich was blessed with a slightly rolling topography and an abundance of sandy loam soil. The ground was easily worked and very fertile, which made farming extremely profitable. There was an abundance of water resources, and the township was nearly divided in half by Raccoon Creek. Various mills can be seen here, including Warrington's mill, Russell's mill, Oliphant's mill, and Vanderbilt's mill. Many of the landowners indicated are descendants of the early Swedish settlers: Hendrickson, Lock, Justice, and Longacre. For good measure, the English families who mixed in with the Swedes prior to the Revolutionary War are also well represented: Lippincott, Batten, Kirby, Davidson, and Black. Woolwich has long welcomed immigrants from distant shores. It has grown and improved by the lasting contributions of each group of settlers.

DISCOVER THOUSANDS OF LOCAL HISTORY BOOKS FEATURING MILLIONS OF VINTAGE IMAGES

Arcadia Publishing, the leading local history publisher in the United States, is committed to making history accessible and meaningful through publishing books that celebrate and preserve the heritage of America's people and places.

Find more books like this at
www.arcadiapublishing.com

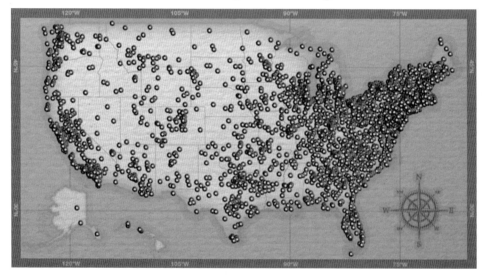

Search for your hometown history, your old stomping grounds, and even your favorite sports team.